The King Bird

Text by A. H. Benjamin
Pictures by Tony Ross

There was once a king who loved birds. He had thousands and thousands of them of almost every species. And they all lived in his palace as free as birds could be.

As one can imagine, they were a nuisance to all the occupants of the palace — except the king, of course.

One day the queen decided that she had had enough. One way or the other, the birds must leave the palace!

So she told the king.

"What!" he cried, horrified. "My birds leave the palace?" He shook his head firmly. "Out of the question!"

"But the place is swarming with them!" protested the queen.

"They're driving me and everyone else mad. Shoo!" she shouted when a pigeon came to perch on her head. "See what I mean? Please, dear," she tried to coax, "be sensible . . . ."

"No!" The king was adamant.

Without another word, the queen stormed out of the throne room.

"I'll get rid of them," she decided, shooing birds right and left as she strode along the corridor.

And no later than that afternoon she found a solution. "Of course!" she thought. "The king's magician is away for the day. I could easily get into his work room. Then...."

A few minutes later she was in the magician's work room, hurriedly leafing through the pages of a book of spells.

"Ah, here it is!" she cried. "How-To-Make-Birds-Disappear," she read, and a triumphant smile lit up her face . . . .

Next day the birds had completely and mysteriously vanished. There wasn't so much as a feather left in the palace to show that they had ever lived there.

The king was distraught.

"My birds! Gone! Vanished!" he wailed, pacing to and fro in the courtyard and waving his arms helplessly. "Where have they disappeared to?"

"How should I know?" replied the queen with a shrug. She pretended to look innocent.

The king suddenly stopped pacing to and fro and stared at his wife suspiciously.

"Don't look at me like that!" she retorted. "I've nothing to do with it!" And she walked briskly away.

But the king was not to be fooled. He knew the queen was somehow responsible, and he wasn't going to forgive her.

"I'll find a way to get my own back on her," he promised himself.

Two days later he had a great idea: he would ask his magician to turn him into a bird!

"Ho, ho!" the king chuckled to himself, delighted with his brainwave. "The queen will love it when she finds out that she has a bird for a husband!"

At first the magician was doubtful when the king told him about his idea but in the end he agreed.

"Very well, Your Majesty," he said. He at once produced his book of spells and set to work.

He wasn't really a clever magician, so it wasn't surprising that the spell did not work properly.

"Oh, dear," he said, dismayed.

The king looked at himself. From the waist down he remained the same; the rest of him, however, had turned into a colourful bird, with a golden crest and a purple beak almost a foot long.

"I like it even better!" he cried, flapping his wings with delight. "This way I can walk like a man and fly like a bird!"

Some time later the king was flying high above the palace.

"What a marvellous feeling flying is," he thought gleefully. "No wonder birds are such happy creatures."

Just then he spotted the queen, hurriedly walking across the courtyard.

"Ah-ha!" he exclaimed. "I think I'll go and say hello." And he swooped down, a sly grin on his bird face.

Silently, he landed behind the queen.

"Hi!" he said, and flapped his wings loudly.

Startled, the queen swung round. "Aaagh!" she screamed, a terrified look on her face. "Aaagh!" She bolted across the courtyard as if pursued by the devil.

The king doubled up with laughter. "Hoo! Hoo! Hoo! The look on her face!"

The terrified queen did not stop running until she reached the royal bedroom.

"What on earth was that?" she panted, her back against the door.

"Only me, dear," replied the king as he came in through the window. "How do you like the new look of your husband?" He began to strut along the room.

Aghast, the queen could not speak.

"Y-you're m-my husband?" she stammered at last.

"Of course," was the reply.

"What have you done to yourself?" she demanded, not at all amused. And when the king told her, she said, "Well, you can just go back to your magician and ask him to restore you to your proper self! I'm not having ... er, er ... a monster as a husband!"

"A monster!" The king pretended to be hurt. "Nonsense. Anyway, I don't wish to argue with you now. It's time for food." He clacked his beak rapidly. "Mm, I fancy some nice, juicy worms."

"Worms!" cried the queen, shocked. "Are you mad?"

"That's what birds eat," replied the king calmly. "Cheerio!" With a flutter of wings he flew out of the window, leaving the queen fuming with indignation.

"Oghh! He can't do that to me!" She knew he was trying to get his own back on her.

That evening when she walked into the royal bedroom, to her horror she found that the king had built a huge nest on his side of the bed. And he was sitting in it!

"What's the idea of building a nest on our bed?" she demanded furiously. "Get rid of it — now!"

His wings folded and his eyes shut, the king didn't take any notice of her.

"Didn't you hear me?" she shouted. "Get rid of that nest!"

The king behaved as if she weren't there, although he was on the verge of bursting with laughter.

Giving up, the queen finally slipped into her side of the bed.

It took her a long time to drop off to sleep, and when she did she had nightmares. She dreamed she was being chased by thousands of birds led by the king. "Caa! Caa! Caa!" they squawked as they chased her along the palace corridors.

Suddenly the queen woke up, sweating and trembling. "Caa! Caa! Caa!" she heard. For a moment she thought she was still dreaming. Then she realised that it was her husband who was making the noise.

"Will you stop making that horrible noise?" she yelled, her hands over her ears. "What do you think you're playing at? It's hardly five o'clock in the morning."

"Birds rise early," replied the king cheerfully. "And I'm joining in the dawn chorus. Caa! Caa! Caa!"

Unable to stand the noise any longer, the queen stormed out of the bedroom, muttering furiously to herself.

Later on, in the dining-hall, the king ordered spaghetti for lunch.

"But you don't like spaghetti," said the queen, surprised.

"I used not to," replied the king, "but I do now. Maybe it's because I'm half bird."

And when a huge plate of spaghetti was placed in front of him, he dived straight into it, picking one strand after the other with his long beak and gulping them down very quickly.

Her face twisted with disgust, the queen watched him eat until he had emptied his plate.

"Mm, that was absolutely delicious!" he said, clacking his beak with delight. "Reminds me so much of worms."

"You're utterly revolting!" said the queen, and she left the table, her food untouched.

Inwardly, the king was bubbling with pleasure.

Next day the queen reminded her husband about the fancy dress party which they were to hold in the palace that evening.

"What are we going to do?" she cried in a panic. "I mean you can't show yourself as you are. What would the guests say?"

"I couldn't care less about the guests," replied the king. "It's my party and I'm going to be in it."

Seeing that the king was not to be dissuaded, the queen said, "All right then. It's a fancy dress party after all. You could always say that you're wearing a costume."

At the party that evening everyone marvelled at the king's costume. "How real it looks!" they said admiringly. "And original too."

The king kept telling them that he wasn't wearing a costume; he was really half man half bird. But, of course, they did not believe him. They thought he had had too much wine to drink and he was only joking.

However, they did believe him when he started flying about and squawking like a mad parrot, creating havoc among the guests. The ladies screamed and the men cursed as they all struggled to leave the ball room.

The poor queen nearly tore her hair out with shame.

"You're making my life a misery," she sobbed, when they were alone again. "You're ten times worse than your birds. I wish I had never got rid of them!"

"So you admit it was you!" exclaimed the king. "I knew it all along! What have you done with them?" he demanded, and the queen told him.

"But I can bring them back," she said wiping the tears away.

"Can you?" cried the king excitedly.

"Yes. All I have to do is to read the magic words backwards and they will reappear instantly. But — can't they live somewhere else?" she pleaded. "I mean you could always build them an aviary in the palace gardens. I'm sure they'll be just as happy living there."

Just the thought of seeing his feathered friends again made the king agree at once. "I think it's a good idea," he said. "It's a deal."

Delighted, the queen hugged him. "Thank you, dear," she said. "Thank you."

"It's all right," smiled the king. "I should've thought about an aviary a long time ago. By the way," he added, winking at her. "I never touched a worm. And I still hate spaghetti!"